My Little Toys

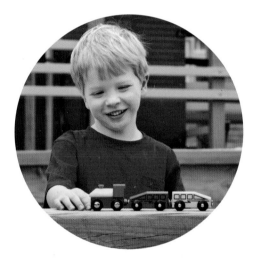

by Jay Dale

This truck is big.

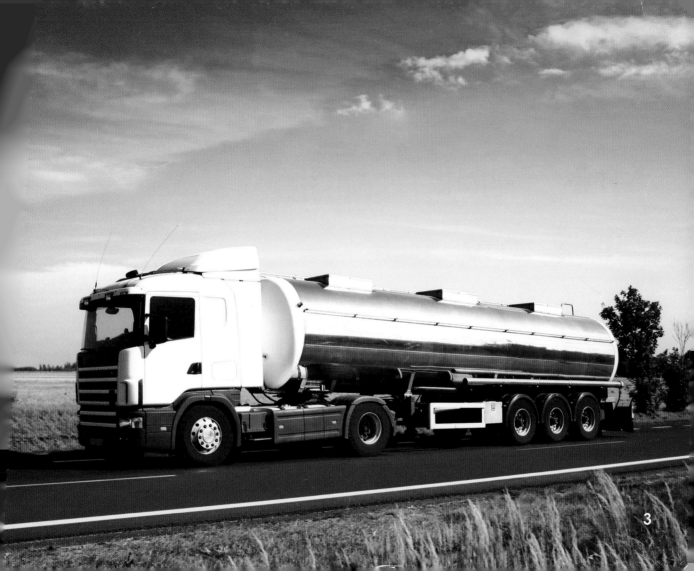

This truck is little.
It is my truck.

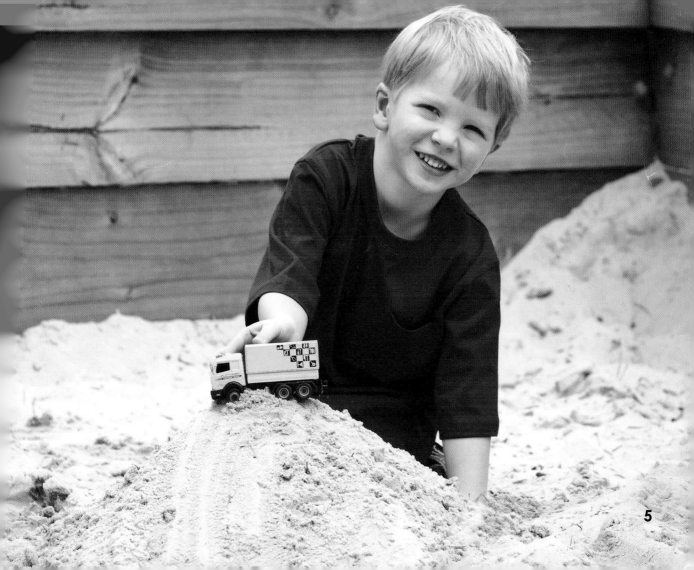

This boat is big.

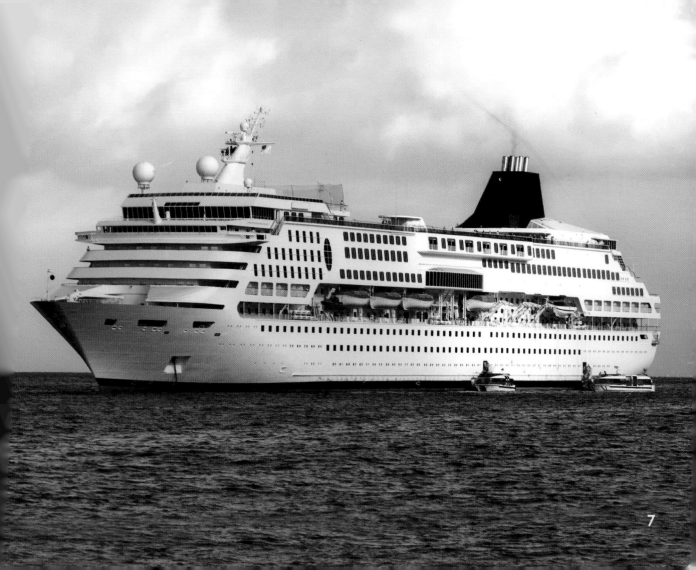

This boat is little.
It is my boat.

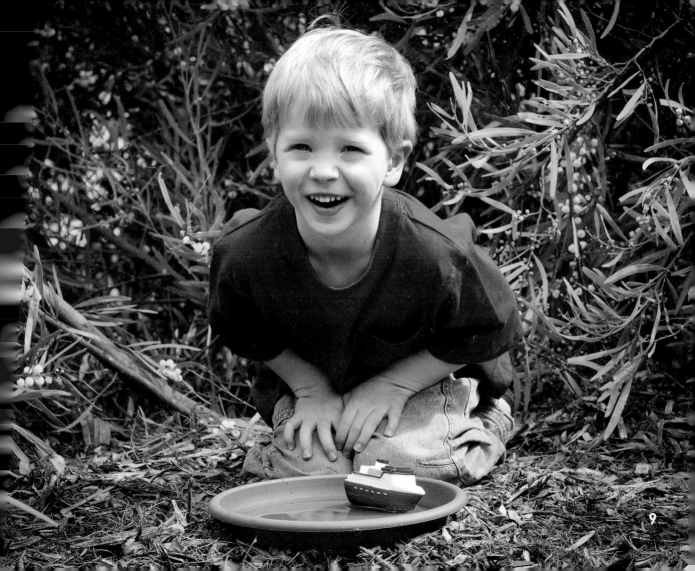

This train is big.

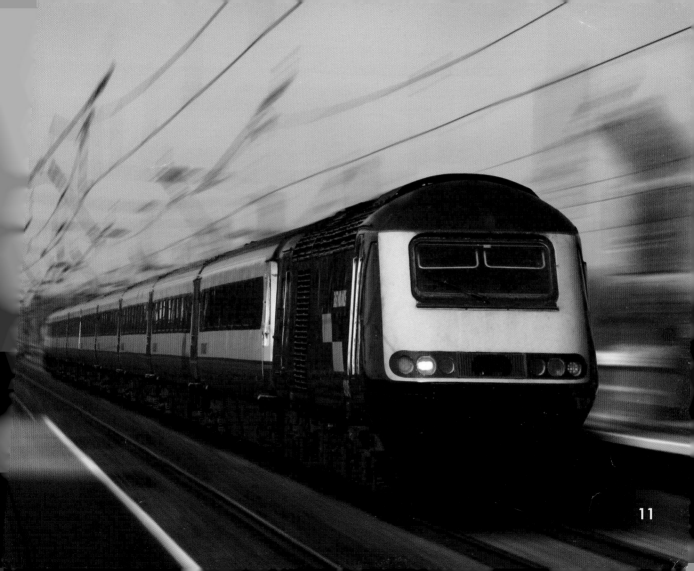

This train is little.
It is my train.

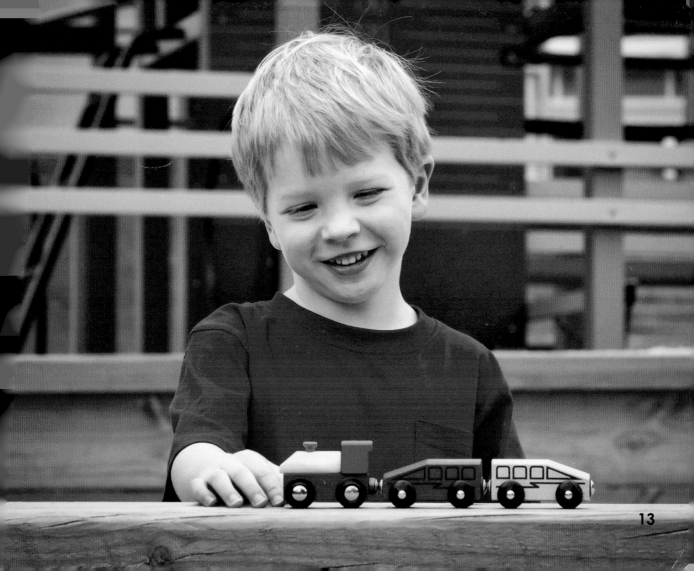

This plane is big.